BONDING

with *Your* RESCUE

DOG

BONDING

with *Your* RESCUE

DOG

Decoding and Influencing Dog Behavior

A Gentle Approach to Understanding and Influencing Canine Behavior

(*Dog Training and Dog Care Series - Book 1*)
Vikk Simmons

Ordinary Matters Publishing

Copyright Information

Bonding with Your Rescue Dog: Decoding and Influencing Dog Behavior (Dog Training and Dog Care Series, Book 1)

Ordinary Matters Publishing
www.Ordinary Matters Publishing.com

Printed in the United State of America
1st print edition: February 2017

Book Layout ©2014 BookDesignTemplates.com
Interior photo credits:
Girl Kissing Dog and *Dog at Barn* by Tim Heitman
Author bio photo by Cynthia Nesser
All other photographs by Vikk Simmons.

BONDING with *YOUR* RESCUE DOG / Vikk Simmons--1st Ed.
ASIN: B00IGJFJZI (eBook)
ISBN-10: 1-941303-27-7 (print)
ISBN-13: 978-1-941303-27-6 (print

Your Thank-you Gift

I'm delighted that you have purchased my book *BOND-ING WITH YOUR RESCUE DOG: Decoding and Influencing Dog Behavior.* As a thank-you, here is your bonus gift. Grab your 27-page free Dog Training and Resource Guide now.

http://www.alifewithdogs.com/a-life-with-dogs-free-gift/

Great for puppies, new dogs, and as a refresher for all other dogs.

Praise for *Easy Homemade Dog Treat Recipes*

"I am impressed by the wealth of information . . . this book would be a great resource for any dog owner, your dog will love you for it." — ML Fitz (Amazon)

"I learned a lot of important DO's and DON'Ts when it comes to healthy feeding of the pets we love". — Dan DeFigio (Amazon)

"This book is a must be read for any dog owner." — Midge (Amazon)

Praise for *Bonding with Your Rescue Dog*

"Highly recommended to all dog lovers as well as those considering adopting a dog!" — Anne (Amazon)

This book details what will be needed after you pick your new pet, how to look after them, what to expect from them, and of course, how to bond with them." — Amy Ryan (Amazon)

"— a must for first time owners and should be read by everyone thinking of adopting a new dog." — Walter Kane (Amazon)

"A very enjoyable book to read and very well written." — Lysanne P. (Amazon)

"Useful information about dog behaviors (and how to change them.) — Cathy Stucker (Amazon Vine)

This book is dedicated to *all* my dogs who were rescued in one manner or another, and especially to my beloved Beau, Jeremiah, Samih, Waco the Wonder Dog, Samwise Samchild, and, most recently, my precious Teddy. Nor can I forget my daily companions: sweet Freddie, goofy Riley, silly Max, pouty Charlie the Pug, and the ever lovely HoneyBunn.

You can meet them all at A Life with Dogs.

www.ALifeWithDogs.com

www.facebook.com/ALifeWithDogs

Insert a favorite photo of your dog here.

"Petting, scratching, and cuddling a dog could be as soothing to the mind and heart as deep meditation and almost as good for the soul as prayer."

—DEAN KOONTZ

Content

Two weeks after I was born, our Asta, the German Shepherd dog who accompanied my dad to Germany and to Korea where he was stationed after World War II, had twelve pups. Decades later, I am still surrounded by dogs.

My first babysitter was a dog. Asta guarded me as I sat in my playpen on the front yard. My first best friend was a dog. As an Army brat without any siblings, our dogs were my earliest and constant companions.

Today my friends and acquaintances often comment on the varied personalities of my dogs and how individual they are. Riley the Cocker Spaniel rock hound is a geologist by trade and loves to bring the best of his river rock finds into the house to decorate his crate. Charlie the Pug can't go an hour without putting on his pouty face about something. Teddy the Shih Tzu and leader of the pack does his best to keep his pack in line but he draws the line with the two cats. Sam, known as the stretch-Cadillac of the Great Pyrenees, demands attention with his noble look, yet all the while he keeps an eye to the sky in search of low-flying planes and helicopters whose appearance sets him off on a gallop leaping into the sky to catch their tails and pull those planes to the ground. There's also a certain amount of fun and pride when walking Sam as we venture down the street, as people seem to think I'm walking a big white horse. Cars slow down, people stare.

Of course Sam is nothing without HoneyBunn the four-pound Mi-Ki who is his ever-present scout watching the sky lanes above. Freddie the Maltese spins and twirls and does his best to garner attention with his dancing bear routine. All are entertained by our newest pack member, Max, the three-year old Great Pyrenees who's become the scourge of neighborhood cats.

Each has made his or her way to my home and into my heart. They are distinct and they are a joy. I am the one who has been rescued.

This book is one small way I can show my gratitude and perhaps help other rescues who are in need of their own forever home.

Science is finally proving what all dog lovers have known for ages. Dogs bring love to their human companions along with some special health benefits. Dogs can provoke a change in mood from sadness to joy in an instant. Feeling their soft nuzzle or stroking them can help lower *YOUR* blood pressure. Listening to their soft snores can bring calm and a sudden smile. Dogs give back in more ways than you can imagine if you just give them a chance.

Vikk Simmons

February, 2014
Houston, Texas

Riley, the Cocker Spaniel, sitting on a picnic table.

ACKNOWLEDGEMENTS

This book was inspired not only by my dogs but by the many dog lovers I've met over the years, especially those who give their time, love, and homes to rescue dogs. Many thanks to the Texas Great Pyrenees Rescue (TGPYR) for introducing me to Waco the Wonder Dog and now Samwise Samchild, the stretch Cadillac of Pyrs. Extra thanks go to Lisa B. who continues to be the foster mother extraordinaire of both my lovely Pyrs. Thank you for making it possible for these noble dogs to enter my home and my heart.

A great debt of gratitude is owed to Claudia B. whose knowledge and experience added much to the development of this book. Also thanks to Cyn M. whose Facebook postings about the non-stop work done by Airedale Rescue Group are a constant amazement. A heartfelt thank-you to all the wonderful veterinarians who have provided such good care for my dogs with an extra nod to Dr. H.

My thanks to all those friends, old and new, who were so instrumental in making this book a reality. Thank you one and all.

Introduction

Go ahead, if you must. Go ahead and tell me that I'm wrong. I admit that I'm biased: I favor rescues over any other dogs. After all, I currently share my home with a slew of them now. When it comes to the question of where and how to get a dog, I think that, as often as possible, people should go out and adopt a dog that needs a forever home. There are a million all over the world. Yet, when it comes to dog options, as easy as they are, we tend to overlook the importance of deeply understanding the adopted dog's past experiences.

It may come as no surprise to you that it was my very own rescues that inspired me to create Bonding With *Your* Rescue Dog. It would be superficial to suggest that all rescue dogs are similar, but I couldn't believe more strongly that, when you find and adopt that special one that becomes your furry best friend, with all his fears, joy, shyness, devotion and perhaps quirkiness, to understand these canine emotions is to understand dogs. It is definitely motivating.

Understanding your duties and responsibilities is the first step in deciding whether to adopt a dog. All dogs require a large amount of time, space, supervision, love, patience, training, veterinary care, healthy nutrition and exercise. It definitely helps if a dog is chosen with love and with the dog's temperament in mind, and with limited assistance from the brain.

There is no breed that is "best" for you. Many mixed breeds may be nippers or aggressive, or fearful of strangers wearing hats at the dog park. To be honest, selecting your shelter dog is something that just happens, quite like falling in love. Sometimes they simply show up on your doorstep. I met a lovable furry dog outside a bowling alley and he became Jeremiah, my friend and companion, for a number of years. He sat outside the bowling alley's main door for three days and I couldn't take it anymore. No one claimed him, but he had somehow managed to claim me.

Rescue dogs will stretch your hearts and fill them with love and compassion. They will awaken the knowledge that there are so many dogs in shelters and with rescue groups waiting to give you all their love, yearning to be rescued and given a second chance. The hope that you see in a dog's eyes when you visit a shelter or meet your new furry friend through a rescue group, and the lift in your own heart in response, is what adoption is all about.

When you've decided that the time is right and you're ready to adopt your new furry best friend, the best way to determine the right fit for your family is to visit your local shelter or contact a local rescue group. Talk to the people who work at the shelter or with the group. Although a large percentage of rescue dogs are mixed breeds, all dogs, no matter their breed or the mix, are unique and have unique personalities and quirks.

Many future pet parents go online in search of the perfect dog to adopt. There are national registries like Petfinder.com that provide photos and brief histories of the available dogs. That's how I found my beloved Great Pyrenees, Waco the Wonder Dog. The people who are closest to the dogs, such as the workers and volunteers with the shelters and rescue groups, or even the foster parents of the dog, can provide you with some of the dog's unique characteristics.

Every furry rescue will need to be walked, and will have different exercise needs, as well as emotional needs. Before adopting your new best friend, be honest with yourself about your lifestyle. Bring home a dog that has the same energy level that you do. Keep in mind that canine companions are "forever companions," and that this is a lifelong commitment to your dog and to all of his health, medical, nutritional, training and exercise needs and quirks.

Rescue dogs often suffer from anxiety and depression, and will need an adjustment period. Some rescue dogs take longer to adapt, while others fit right in. But what happens when your newly adopted canine companion won't stop barking, is terrified of other dogs and people, growls at your children or won't leave the cats' food alone? Sometimes training an older rescue can be more challenging, but not impossible.

Training our canine companions should never be stressful. Instead it should be fun and inspiring for both you and your dog. The benefits of positive training are huge. Positive training not only strengthens your bond with your dog, but also teaches you empathy, patience, and compassion. You'll learn how to understand your dog and what really drives him to do the things he does. Training should not be about power and dominance. When using the positive approach, you will start observing some rather interesting behaviors. All dogs are keen to learn. They all want to be praised and rewarded. So forget the old stuff. Punishment doesn't have a place here when training rescues or any dogs for that matter.

Teddy, the Shih Tzu and alpha dog of my pack.

Getting In Touch With Your Adopted Dog

5 Things to Know Before Adoption

Adopting the perfect puppy or adult dog is most often done after deciding which puppy most fits your personality. Each puppy is unique. Perhaps you are most likely to prefer a Labrador because he has the calmest temperament or a German Shepherd/mix because you envision yourself going for those afternoon jogs. Either way, the most reliable way of finding out about your dog's temperament is by spending time at a shelter. Each and every dog has a particular personality based upon past experience, environmental factors, and inherited genes.

Spend a little time watching various types of dogs. When you think you have an idea of a particular breed or mix, go online and research the breed characteristics to see if they'd be a good fit for you and your lifestyle. Read magazine articles and check out a few books. Get a feel for the type of dog you'd like and how they would fit into your daily life. Sometimes you might remember a type of dog that you encountered earlier in your life, and that will point you in a direction.

I remember the Cocker Spaniel my grandmother had when I was growing up. Mitzi was her name. She was a lovable, cute blonde spaniel, and she seeded a love for Cockers in my heart. Many years later I received a call from a friend who'd seen a stunning black Cocker Spaniel in the window of a local department store as part of an Adoption Day event. She called and I found myself on the way to claim that lovable boy. Today Riley, a blonde Cocker Spaniel, is one of my current pack of lovable companions. They are wonderful dogs.

Small gains contribute to your dog's emotional growth. This doesn't happen in a day. All dogs have good qualities. Some are friendlier than others. Some have high activity levels and need more exercise than others. Many behaviors need to be generalized outside the home, so if your rescue is great at home and nervous at the dog park, keep going and doing all the things that your furry best friend enjoys. Encourage the right behavior in your dogs and understand the long-term value in changing the negative ones.

Selecting a Breed: Mixed Breeds Make Wonderful Family Pets

Most shelters and rescue groups have many dogs and puppies to choose from. You can use puppy testing and your own judgment to match puppies and people. Selecting a friendly and helpful shelter is done very easily. Each breed has certain characteristics. Remember, it is important to understand that each breed/mix looks different and behaves differently. Do not, however, stereotype a dog according to his breed.

Most dogs will have many of the characteristics of their particular breed, yet past experiences, such as trauma, illness, abuse, and even frequently changing homes will alter a dog's behavior or reactions to different external stimuli such as noise, other dogs and people, and children.

Dogs, like children, are always learning. Expose your rescue dogs to new experiences, including playing with other dogs. Playing involves many different behaviors like stalking, chasing, play-fighting, socializing, and having fun. Long walks in your neighborhood will expose him to children on bikes, babies in strollers, and strangers wearing hats. Your rescue will slowly show signs of improvement. His fragile inner self will soon become confident as he has you by his side.

Visualize the Adult Dog

Puppies are known for their playfulness and, when little, are easy to manage. Nonetheless, visualizing how large your puppy will become as an adult, and how he will behave physically and behaviorally when he matures is just as important.

Dogs and Exercise

Matching your personality and energy levels with a particular breed/mix prepares you for your dog's activity level. Do you enjoy lounging around with your furry-best friend and a good book? Or does the idea of going to the dog beach with a Frisbee seem more favorable? Watching how puppies behave in a litter will give you much more information on whether he is shy, relaxed, or energetic. Is he an Alpha pup? All dogs and puppies express emotions, including fear, shyness, aggressiveness, or pure happiness. As a future pet parent, it is extremely important to be aware of these emotions when choosing your next furry-best friend.

Talk to the Shelter, Handlers, and Rescue Group Workers

Ask any questions regarding breeding, care, nutrition and temperament, exercise and training. Everyone working at shelters or with rescues will take your needs into consideration and do the perfect match. Often it's best left to the shelter manager to make the final decision. Interpreting a pup's facial expressions, his unique pitch and frequency of the many barks, as well as his body posture and eye expression, allows for all future dog parents to analyze a pup's moods, temperament and how their puppy is feeling at that particular time. By observing pups play within their litter, a future pet parent becomes more in tune with what it is in a puppy that they are looking for. Big or small, energetic or cuddly? This same observation is important for searching out an older dog too.

Deciding on the Best Age

Many people want to adopt puppies instead of adult dogs. Puppies go through a fear period during their eighth week through twelfth week, so it is always recommended that you keep this in mind if they are this age and at a shelter or with a rescue group. Avoid frightening your puppy during this period as this will have a lasting effect on him, more than at any other time in his life.

Adopting an older puppy that is twelve weeks or older necessitates a few more questions. Has the puppy spent time alone with a person on a regular basis for at least six days a week? Has the puppy been socialized and taken out of his pen or kennel, and has he experienced different environments? If not, kennel shyness occurs, and your new puppy will experience behavioral difficulties around people, other dogs and animals. Reputable dog shelters and organizations ensure that sufficient individual attention, puppy training, and socialization is given to all puppies and adult dogs.

Bringing Fido Home

Adoption day arrives, and you finally get to bring Fido home. After all the planning and deciding, you whisk home your new best friend. His entry into the real world is definitely going to have its moments (whose doesn't), but you can make things as comfortable as possible by knowing what to expect, and making a few simple preparations ahead of time.

You've probably heard of "childproofing" — and yes, you're more than likely going to have to do a little or a lot of "puppy proofing" to your home. It's a good idea to limit a new dog's adventures to one or two rooms in your home at the beginning, and then let him earn his freedom throughout the house. Decide right away which parts of the house will be fair game for your dog. Kitchens have always been a favorite since they are easy to clean. They have easy-to-clean tiled floors, and there's usually enough room for play. Don't plan on leaving Fido alone for long periods of time even if he's in the kitchen. Dogs all need company and get bored easily.

Even if your kitchen or other rooms have doors which can be closed, baby gates allow dogs to see and hear you while you're in other parts of the house. They also tend to make your dog feel less like a captive. You're also less likely to worry since you can keep an eye on him without having to open and close doors. Make sure that you pick up everything off the floor and store any wastebaskets out of sight. Remove everything on countertops to prevent even medium-sized dogs from jumping up and snatching foods or spilling hot liquids like coffee or soups on themselves. If you have cabinets at doggie level, cover all corners and handles with childproofing locks and covers to prevent injury to your dog. This also discourages chewing.

Most dangerous are the cleaning products and other chemicals, which should be stored and locked away. Sharp utensils that can pose a danger should also be placed in a safe place. Once your new dog learns all the rules within your home and has settled down, things will be more relaxed, and you can slowly organize things back to the way they were. Some dogs will never shred a carpet or piece of furniture, while others will delight in playing around almost like a bored child.

Now that you've "baby proofed" your home, make sure that you've made a list of all the supplies that you will be needing. Some like the leash or crate will prove useful right from the start.

Crate

Having a crate doesn't mean that this needs to be used all the time. It's useful for housebreaking, traveling, bedtime, and when you're having guests or repairmen over and need to keep Fido confined for a short period of time. If your dog is still a puppy and has some growing to do, think ahead and purchase a crate that he can grow into.

Dogs, like humans, value their freedom at all costs. Think of crating in this way. Do you think it's mean to keep your child in a playpen for a couple of hours each day? Dogs are den animals that most enjoy being safe and having a space to call their own. A crate should never be used because you're too lazy to go out for a walk or because your dog is not behaving. Crates need to be used judiciously. It's a way of keeping your furry best friend safe and out of harm's way.

Baby Gates

The baby gate is very useful in keeping puppies, even adult dogs, restricted to certain areas in your home. Baby gates can be used temporarily, and when your dog gets older and can be trusted around the house, all the gates can be removed. These are great for preventing unwanted behaviors around the house such as chewing your favorite rugs, or even being in the same part of the house as your cats.

Management tools help you to manage your dog's behavior. They make it easier for you to teach your dog that only desirable behaviors make good things happen right away. With the proper training tools, dogs don't have the opportunity to misbehave, because management tools help prevent unwanted behaviors before they even start.

Exercise Pen

Often, a collapsible and portable pen comes in handy. It is a sturdy wire pen that you can put your furry best friend in and will keep him safely under wraps. These are great for puppies and small dogs.

Leash and Collar

There are definite necessities like leashes and collars. Leashes should be four to six feet long, and made of either cotton, nylon or leather. No chain or plastic allowed. Retractable leashes are not recommended as it takes a while to get proficient with them. Get two collars: one for training and one for around the house. Never leave a "choke chain" on your dog when he's unsupervised since a dog can get hurt if his collar gets attached to something. Check the collar every few weeks to make sure that it's not too tight.

Food and Food and Water Bowls

Consult with your veterinarian as to the best types of food for your dog, and on how much to feed him. Introduce his new diet gradually by combining his old feed with the new feed in gradual doses.

Beds and Bedding

All dogs appreciate comfortable, non-allergenic plush beds that they can cuddle in. Rectangular doggie mats also work if combined with a folded-up blanket. These fit perfectly into crates and are easy to take along when traveling.

Grooming Tools

All grooming tools are absolute necessities for your dogs. A bath is going to be one of the first things on Fido's agenda, so choosing a chemical-free dog shampoo, preferably organic, brings great results.

Dog Toys

Interactive dog toys keep boredom at bay. Go for sturdy and safe toys that your dog can't choke on or destroy. Knotted rope bones are wonderful. Never give old shoes or clothes: he may think that it's okay to have a chew on other shoes and clothes.

A young Teddy tasting a plant.

Resources and Items Needed

_____

_____

_____

_____

_____

_____

_____

_____

_____

_____

_____

_____

_____

_____

_____

_____

_____

_____

_____

_____

_____

_____

_____

_____

_____

_____

_____

_____

_____

_____

_____

_____

_____

What To Expect When Bringing Fido Home

Some newly adopted dogs love human contact, but on the other hand, have mixed feelings about meeting new people or children. Some may act like "Cujo," but settle down after a couple of days. Others may remain timid, and roll over on their backs, but react negatively to a belly rub. Many adopted dogs take a few weeks to reveal their true temperaments. Dogs, like people are complicated, and all the variables that have painted their past come into play within the first few months after adoption. Aging dogs often come with chronic pain from arthritis or illness, and will be more sensitive to people touching them or going for long walks. Many mature dogs may develop dementia, which often times bring on dramatic changes in personality.

Behaviors to Expect

Barking uncontrollably when left alone or when excited or scared
Hyperactivity
Fearfulness and insecure most times
Shyness
Chewing on objects
Aggressiveness towards people, children and other animals
Pulling on the leash
Not walking on the leash
Fearfulness of strangers, children and other pets
Nervousness around the house
Vomiting from stress
Disliking being groomed or bathed
Sleeping for long periods of time
Canine Depression
Post Traumatic Stress Disorder
Fear of noises
Fear of feet
Fear of hands or hand motions
Fear of Anyone Touching Him
Fear of eating or drinking
Destruction of furniture, carpets or objects
Food Guarding
Toy Guarding
Bed Guarding
Fear of the veterinarian

Many of these typical behavior problems behaviors may not be present in your rescue. Those that are present can be solved easily. Identify the problems that your dog has. Many dogs lie on their backs to indicate that they pose no threat to anyone. However, it can mean that they would like for the person touching them to go away, or, paradoxically, to stay. When people misread the intended communication given by a rescue dog, these dogs may bite. Relaxed dogs all have "soft" eyes. There is no tension and the dog will be in a relaxed state physically. A focused "stiff" gaze should alert the new dog owner that his furry companion is tense, and may be feeling defensive and vulnerable.

Give your adopted dog time to adapt to his new home. Remember that this is all new to him, and that the change in environment from the shelter to a private home may cause him tension. Many shelter dogs will yawn when exposed to a new situation. A rescue dog that is anxious may pace or circle around. Sometimes rolling over may demonstrate that your dog is trying to diffuse a tense situation, possibly with another dog. Watch out for the tucked-in tail and stiff mouth, indicating that he is stressed and anxious. Tucked-in tails could also be an involuntary physical response that is hardwired into your dog's neural pathway. That's why it takes a few weeks or even months to really get to know your newly adopted dog.

If your dog has many behavioral issues — loud barking, lunging, or growling, contact your veterinarian so that you can develop a balanced and trusting relationship with your dog.

Transition Time

So now you've "puppy-proofed," or "dog proofed" your home and filled it up with all things Fido. On your way to the shelter, bring the leash, harness, and a crate for the car. Bring someone along that can hold your dog or puppy in the back seat if you don't have a traveling crate.

By no means have a Welcome Home party. The huge transition for your dog will be less upsetting if you keep everything as calm as possible when you get home. This is definitely not the time to have a party or to invite a whole group of friends over. Rather do all the invites in a week or two when Fido has settled into his new home and things are starting to run smoothly.

Names and Other Identifiers

If your dog already has a name that he goes by and that you like, keep it. But if you need to choose one, pick something trendy and fun. Keep in mind that you'll be calling out to him at the dog park, or when out and about, and you don't want something that sounds ridiculous. Order name tags and make sure that your name, address and phone number are clearly marked. Always have some form of identification on your dog in case he runs off. Visit your veterinarian and microchip as soon as possible. It's vital that this is done as soon as possible. Most dogs in shelters and with rescue groups are lost dogs that did not have any form of ID on them.

Riley enjoying his lounge pillow.

Things to Remember

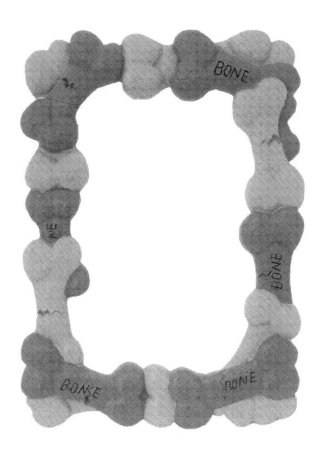

The First Day and Night with Fido

DAY ONE

Visit Your Veterinarian

Most rescues are terrified of the veterinarian, and will seek comfort from you. Keep him away from other dogs until you know how he reacts around other dogs and cats. Explain to your vet where and when you adopted him, his current feed, fears, and behaviors and in particular, what vaccinations he's had. Ask as many questions as you can. Don't be shy. Choosing a veterinarian is rather like choosing a pediatrician. There will be times that you may need to come see your vet late at night or just have a phone call returned. Make the most of your relationship with your veterinarian, and don't hesitate to send over a thank you note with some flowers.

Introduce Your New Dog to the Home and to the Family

When you first get home, take your time to show your dog around your garden and your home, but don't introduce him just yet to the other dogs in your home or to the neighbor's pets. Bring him inside and calmly introduce him to the rest of the family. Don't yell or crowd him and keep little children from grabbing hold of him or running around. Take a few minutes and allow for each family member to greet him gently. Next show him the room where he'll be settling in, and food bowls that should have fresh water and fresh food. Show him his toys and crate and that special blanket that you've selected especially for him.

Give Your Dog a Bath

You'll most likely want to give him a bath in your bathtub, possibly a flea bath if necessary. Wipe out his ears with an alcohol swab - one for each ear — and try to introduce him to a doggie toothbrush by brushing his teeth gently with doggie toothpaste made especially for dogs. He'll be delighted at how great he feels after a good grooming.

Don't Overfeed Your New Dog

If he has not eaten since the shelter, he may want a meal. Keep that meal small since travel and being in a new environment may cause an upset stomach. Don't watch him eat, since this will stress him out even more.

Dogs that have changed environments and are nervous may be prone to diarrhea for the first few days. If this persists, try cooking some brown rice and shredded boiled chicken. You could even try hand feeding when cooled, in case he's too nervous to eat. It's not uncommon for dogs to stop eating when in a new environment. Calm environments, calming music, and homemade food tend to relieve any symptoms of nervousness.

Establish a Good Potty Routine

That said, it's important to remember to bring him outside to relieve himself and start to develop a schedule as soon as possible.

Keep Your New Dog Close to You at Night

For the first few weeks, you can bring his crate next to your bed until he gets used to being in your home and has settled in. Dogs love company, and by being close to you, he will be able to seek comfort or reassurance that everything is okay. You'll most likely love his presence too. He'll probably end up on your bed. There's nothing better than having your furry best friend snuggle up next to you in the cold winter months. Keep in mind that many dog experts recommend crating right from the beginning, so that he may not challenge your authority as pack leader.

Introducing "The Crate"

Start by introducing your dog to the crate slowly. Use a toy or food treat to welcome her into the crate. Verbal encouragement needs to be soothing. You should use a phrase that you will always use to get him to enter his crate — "Go in your crate. Good Boy." In this way, your dog will eventually learn what is expected of him.

In the beginning, keep your crate fairly free of too many toys. Some shelter dogs may chew up everything inside or relieve themselves inside the crate. Nonetheless, there are some dogs that are used to being crated. In the case of your dog reacting unhappily to being confined to a crate, take each step slowly and patiently. You'll only make matters worse if you get angry or impatient.

Chances of success increase if you encourage and reward each step of the way. Remember that crating is not a punishment and that the crate should be used for only short periods of time. Start with a few seconds several times a day, and then gradually increase to minutes.

Dogs Often Love Their Crates

My huge Great Pyrenees, Sam, loves his crate. Every day at one o'clock, he willingly goes to his crate and waits for me to let him in for his afternoon nap. I think he's happy to have some alone time from his canine brothers. At night he's more than willing to go to bed as he knows his bedtime treats await.

I have a smaller crate in the den where we spend much of our time. Periodically, throughout the day, Teddy, the Shih Tzu, will toddle off to the crate where he naps and simply separates himself from the other dogs. I've also noticed that Riley, the Cocker Spaniel, will go into the crate to rest, particularly when his knee and hip are acting up. They seem to find the crate comforting and don't look at it as a negative at all.

Don't expect your new dog to remain in his crate for a few hours, especially if he has not been housebroken yet. Many veterinarians and shelters recommend keeping your dogs confined for no longer than 4 hours. Some suggest not using this method at all since it is too confining. Dogs need to stretch their legs and move around.

Remember this: If your dog starts barking or whining in his crate, do **not** give him a treat or biscuit. Rewarding that kind of behavior teaches him that he needs to do just that to get rewarded treat. Instead, and most importantly, reward when he's quiet and relaxed. This may take a while since many shelter dogs suffer from anxiety and fear being alone or enclosed in small spaces. If you're patient and consistent, your dog will learn to treat the crate as his special place.

When your dog becomes trustworthy and relaxed around your home, then you may decide that he does not need to be crated while you're running errands. Dogs get bored easily, so remember to leave some interactive dog toys on his dog bed. If your newly-adopted dog has a mischievous streak or has hit adolescence, do not give him too much freedom, unless he's been out for a long walk and has used up his energy.

How to Leave and Reenter the Home

Leaving home should be done calmly with no hysterical goodbyes. You're teaching your dog to be independent, and that it's okay to be alone. Leave without any emotion or you will clue him in that something is amiss. Arriving back home should pretty much be done in the same way.

Keeping Your Dog Company

The real trick during the first couple of days is assessing your dog's temperament and trying to figure out if he needs constant supervision. No dog is happy being left alone for long periods of time. If you leave any dog alone for too long, they'll get into mischief because they get lonely and bored. This happens to the best of dogs.

Do not follow him around. Give him enough space to feel comfortable. He needs to be able to get along without you at his side, but he also needs to know that you're there for him when he needs that belly rub, walk or cuddle. By allowing your dog to spend time with you, he'll soon know that you're his best friend, protector, and pet parent - which means leader. By being kind and patient, you'll ensure a smooth transition process and allow for a happy, well-balanced dog.

If at all possible, I try to bring new dogs into the home when I know I'm going to be there for a couple of days. Often it's the weekend. I plan ahead so that the first days will be quiet and calm and without friends. That way the dog can acclimate to his surroundings and the home atmosphere more easily.

Charlie the Pug, Freddie the Maltese, and HoneyBunn the Miki
enjoying some down time.

Place a photo of your dog's first day here.

More Memories of Our First Days

Housebreaking

Housebreaking problems are the number one reason that pet parents give up their dogs for adoption. That's sad, since housebreaking does not have to be complicated at all. It can be done in a short period of time if taught consistently. Doggie potty-training can be taught in four simple steps:

Step 1: Scheduling. Develop a firm routine that you stick by no matter what. If your furry best friend knows what to expect and that he'll be taken outside, he soon won't mind waiting until his next scheduled outing. If you take him out at different times, he won't know when it's time, and it's not worth his while waiting or he probably cannot hold himself.

Step 2: If your dog has just had a meal and lots of water, he's going to need to go outside. It's therefore important and necessary that you schedule feed times and keep snacks to a minimum. Fresh water should never be scheduled and should always be available.

Step 3: Timing rules here! Your dog may have accidents. Yes, it's okay. Don't get mad at him, but you can get mad at yourself. Teach him right from wrong gently, and take him outside to correct him. I don't believe that you should stop him mid-potty, but right afterwards. Bladders and bowel movements cannot suddenly come to a stop, so think like a dog and with compassion at all times. Also keep in mind that older dogs often lose bladder control or cannot get outside in time. Discuss this with your veterinarian.

Step 4: Cleanliness is important and it's necessary to keep your home and dog's quarters clean. Dogs always return to their favorite spots. If this happens to be a couch or carpet, thoroughly disinfect to remove all scents. Leave no traces behind. I have also used the new odor and pheromone extractor type cleaners that are now available.

Dog bladder control problems may be related to urinary tract infections, muscle control issues in some spayed dogs, and sometimes even diabetes and kidney problems. Contact your veterinarian if your rescue has a weak bladder. Treatment is uncomplicated with medications. If these don't work then surgery or holistic treatments are often used.

The Case of Charlie the Pug

At six months of age Charlie the Pug showed up on my doorstep when his owner, completely frustrated, dropped him and his crate off for a round of puppy boot camp. The owner complained that Charlie was un-trainable and that he refused to be potty-trained. She insisted that he liked pooping in his crate because he would roll around in it in his crate every day, and then she'd have to clean him and his crate when she got home at night.

I questioned her about her habits caring for Charlie. It didn't take long to figure out that there were several problems at work, and all were controlled by the owner and not little Charlie. Unfortunately, Charlie's new momma did everything backwards. Yes, she would get up and put him outside for his morning potty; but then she would feed him and, instead of allowing him to go potty again she'd put him in the crate and leave for work.

I can't stress enough how important it is to let your dogs outside to potty after they eat. If you do so, it will save you a lot of stress and fuss and also make your dog very happy. What was Charlie to do? He was locked in a crate for hours with a full bladder and a full tummy with food that would have to come out. He did what any little dog would do, he went to the far end of his crate and pottied.

Did Charlie love rolling around in his poo? No. Charlie had a lot of flea bites that created a severe itching problem for him. He was absolutely miserable to the point where he was jumping around in his crate and rubbing against the rungs in order to relieve the itching. This stopped almost immediately after I put him on flea medicine and gave him a nice warm oatmeal bath.

Was Charlie un-trainable? Absolutely not. In fact, he turned out to be one of the easiest little fellows to train that I've ever run across. He's adorable and he definitely has personality. Charlie was a true misunderstood little Pug.

As it turns out, Charlie became the little Pug who came to dinner, and stayed, and stayed, and stayed, and stayed!

Puppy Bladder Control

If your puppy is under six months of age, he will not have full bladder control yet. You'll need to take him outside first thing early morning, and let him have supervised playtime. Next, he'll need to go outside after his morning meal and regularly throughout the day. This will be necessary at least 6-8 times a day, sometimes more. Enjoy your time with him, play ball or enjoy a game of peek a boo. Cover your face with both hands and say, "peek a boo - where's mommy?" Open up your palms and show your face. Your puppy will delight in this form of play.

If your pup has occasional accidents in your home, be gentle. No yelling. You'll want him to be trust you, not be afraid of you. Many new dogs will sit and wait if you turn them outside in your garden. It's necessary to spend the time outside, so that your dog does not become anxious about being locked outside without you. Your job during the housebreaking process is to encourage your dog or puppy to do his business outside, and to keep the house clean.

Later on you can take him on a leash and say, "Go potty." When he relieves himself, make a big fuss and immediately reward him with his favorite treat. Do this each and every time. Bring a treat with you and reward the very second he's done his business outside. Then let him have a long walk, or play off-leash in your backyard.

Never rub your dog's nose in his mess. Never hit or scold a dog if he has an accident. Don't think your dog looks guilty because he's pottied inside. That look is one of fear and something that your dog should never wear. Guilt and sadness all belong back at the shelter. This is the time of new beginnings filled with love and happiness. Remember you're trying to overcome any training mistakes he's had in the past, any forms of abuse he's gone through. This all takes time and patience, but can be done. Think like your dog, and try to understand him and where he has come from. He'll respect you more for that, and become your best friend in no time at all.

All dog training, including housebreaking, depends on consistency and patience. The more you reward his going outdoors, and the more you praise him every time he goes outside, the faster he'll become housebroken. You'll also have a happier dog. Make your weekdays and weekend schedules the same. Dogs do not differentiate between the two. Every day has to be the same.

Write down your schedule and keep it posted on your refrigerator. Remind everyone in your house to participate. Your dog soon may start going to the front door and barking. This is his way of letting you know that it's time. Always respond to his signals. Although some dogs take longer than others, the slower ones will soon catch on. Dogs are smart, and want to please. Give him time, show him the rules, reinforce consistently, and reward!

Have trouble remembering when it's time for "potty time?" Don't always catch the "I-have-go-potty" signal? If you're like me and work at home, or spend a lot of time at home, take advantage of the oven timer or a stand-alone kitchen timer to help you remember to let your dog go outside. I keep the timer far enough away so that I have to get up from the computer or walk over to it in order to turn it off. That way I'm up and the dogs are ready to "go outside" for "potty time."

Teddy daring anyone to take his bon

Housebreaking Tips and Reminders

Use this section to make notes about your dog.

_____

_____

_____

_____

_____

_____

_____

_____

_____

_____

_____

_____

_____

_____

Positive Training

What Makes Positive Training So Effective?

Positive training enables you to get your new furry best friend to perform the behaviors that you want, while rewarding him with treats, food, and toys in return. It means never using physical or verbal punishment on your dogs, and not forcing your dogs to perform a particular behavior through force. When you first adopt a dog and bring him home, not only do you bring a new furry best friend home, but also all his bad habits. Some dogs have never been trained, and don't know what it is that you're asking of them.

While you're both going to enjoy each other's company, there are some things that he may do that will drive you crazy .You already know that by adopting a shelter dog you're bringing home all past experiences that this dog has had. You're also bringing home his fears, sadness and joy. Many dogs that leave shelters are prone to canine depression and post traumatic stress disorder. In this chapter, I'll suggest creative ways to help ease him out of depression and to keep him entertained while he's at home with you.

Make this time the beginning of a beautiful relationship by thinking like your dog, and understanding him and where he's come from, and what experiences he's gone through. Learn to put yourself in his situation. I'll guarantee that after positive training, some organic homemade meals, trips to the dog park and lots of cuddles you'll soon overcome any problems.

Take That First Step

The first step is identifying all the annoying behaviors that you'd like to change. For instance, when one of my dogs was a puppy, he loved to jump up on everyone that walked through the front door. Rather than keep him outside, I decided to use the clicker only when he responded and came to me. When he did come bounding towards me, I clicked and praised him. This was accompanied always by lots of encouragement and tasty treats. After repeating this a few times, he stopped jumping up on the guests and waited in anticipation for treats when the clicks came.

Different behavioral profiles need to be taken into consideration at all times. Understanding your dog's unique character is necessary before any training can succeed. A friendly people-breed such as a retriever will have no problems being around lots of people and other dogs. A shy dog will need a peaceful environment with hardly any distractions. Teaching new behaviors to puppies will take numerous sessions to perfect a new behavior. Sometimes dog owners make mistakes without even realizing, but owing to a dog's resilient nature, small training mistakes hardly result in long-term damage. Nonetheless, consistent training errors will result in years of frustration. Combining training, socialization, enrichment, and love will result in a confident and well-behaved dog.

With positive training, our dogs are never wrong or stupid. What clicker-training has shown is that specific behaviors can be learned. It's all about mental attitude. Happier and more focused dogs have a much easier time learning. We develop stronger relationships, and have far less behavioral problems with POSITIVE TRAINING.

Why is Ignoring Certain Behaviors So Important?

This is easier said than done, but once you start doing this you'll see great results.

First Things First

Completely ignore your dog, even if he's having a great time munching your carpets.

Redirect your dog to an activity than you can positively reinforce.

Use the crate when you find yourself becoming impatient or angry. Never lose your patience or become angry. Leave the room instead. Always show kindness, respect and calm.

Remember to reinforce **only the behavior that you want**. Do not accidently reinforce bad behavior even when you're in a rush. Keep a schedule, a timeline, and a chart. Note down all accomplishments. Join online training websites like pupspace.com to further enhance your training skills. Make use of both training with a registered professional, as well as virtual training online with sites like pupspace.com to reinforce everything you've learned. Virtual dog training websites have become increasingly popular.

Prevent bad situations from happening before they actually happen. Understand your dog and his reactions to other people, children, and other animals. If your dog dislikes children, place him in another room before they arrive. Your dog does not need to be aggravated. Some dogs enjoy tranquility with one or two people around. Others love being around many people, and don't change the way they react to stimuli no matter how much chaos and noise surrounds them.

Reinforcing the Behaviors You Want in Your Rescue

Listing all the existing behaviors that you would like to change in your new rescue makes for easier and longer-lasting changes. You have to know what you want to change. Many frustrating behaviors can easily be changed. Break down each behavior into small easy steps. Write them down. Thirty-second increment training can be effective if the behavior being taught is complicated. When your dog has been continually successful with each step, you can then raise the bar and move on to the next level. Advance each behavior to the next level with lots of praise and treats.

Why Doesn't My Dog Respond to Training?

Some of us may have chosen to adopt an adult dog that has never had prior training. Other pet parents may have neglected to continue with their pup's training, only to find out that with adult dogs, the unwanted behavior is harder to change because it is now an established behavior. Some shelter dogs have come from neglectful homes where they never lounged on a bed, or had consistent training. Although dog shelters and many rescue organizations work with many dogs at shelters, it is hard to change an established behavior over a short period of time.

At times, harnessing an active or aggressive dog's scattered attention and channeling it to specific goals simply does not work. Getting your dog's attention takes patience, kindness, and time. An overall positive and kind mindset needs to be attained so that training can be effective. Ask any dog owner about training difficulties and you'll be sure to hear that different behavioral profiles have to be taken into consideration. Each dog has a unique personality. Each and every dog also has his quirks.

Providing some crating time prior to a training class helps to improve attitude, and can help tone down a hyper or distracted dog. This can only work if he's not distressed and getting worked up. Reward him with a treat when he stops howling and barking in the crate. Do not let him out of the crate when he is barking to get out because you are only reinforcing a negative behavior, one you don't want.

Your dog must know how to behave in and out of the crate. Being able to relax is a valuable and is an important skill for most dogs that are difficult to train.

Reinforce basic obedience! This is more effective when using a leash, or an electronic collar, provided that your dog is conditioned to it. The most important obedience skill to focus on is heel. This sets the tone for your training, workout or trip to the dog park. Do all your training on a leash, so that you can constantly reinforce your training commands.

Good Manners Begins with Basic Training

Several years ago I spent quite a bit of time with a dog trainer who'd been training dogs for more than fifty years. He was also adept at training horses. A few weeks with Pete and he would produce what seemed like miracles in dogs. I wanted to know his secret.

You would think he spent hours and hours with the dogs but he didn't. His training sessions were short, concise, and basic. He did one focused training session every day that lasted five to ten minutes. The secret? He did it daily. He reinforced it during the day during any interaction. When a dog would balk at doing things, Pete would take the dog back to the basics: sit, stay, come, lie down. They would work their way back to the desired goal. He did the training daily, no matter the weather, no matter how he felt. Everyone can spend five minutes working with their dog. Everyone.

Provide mental stimulation for your dog. When you've made progress in the basic obedience field, channel your dog's activeness into a more stimulating world — agility, dock diving, fly ball or field competition. All dogs need to have fun. They tend to respond to training in a more positive way after letting all their energy out in the dog park playing Frisbee.

Be consistent with the rules. Consistency enables you to reshape your dog's behavior and to help him calm down and be respectful during training.

Keep yourself calm at all times. Dogs are masters at reading your body language. You can use the silent treatment and ask your dog to do a long "stay" in the heel position, using a leash, and not say anything for a few minutes. Then give the heel command and start walking. Having the leash on enables you to immediately correct. Resume the training session, when you're done.

Actual training sessions should be kept short, yet fun and rewarding for dogs that don't do well in training. When your dog focuses, make positive use of this attention span and reward him. Most dogs need a reward in order to put on their best effort during training. Positive training always works best. Both pups and fully-grown dogs love treats and plenty of praise.

When your dog responds correctly to training, reward him immediately. Pups and dogs always need to feel that you are their mentors and are always consistent with their training, your behavior, and all teaching methods.

Then give the heel command and start walking. Having the leash on enables you to immediately correct. Resume the training session, when you're done.

How to Stop Your Puppy from Jumping Up

Different dogs will present different challenges. Most puppies will enjoy jumping up to greet you. Every adopted puppy or dog arrives with their own unique set of person-ality quirks-most of them great ones that you'll sooner or later learn to accept. Remember not every quirk needs to be changed.

Having your new puppy jump up on you or visitors can be annoying, and also dangerous for small children. So for most of us, there's no denying the benefits of obedience classes for our canine companions.

Training your pooch to behave well in your home is ac-tually so much easier than most people think. However, certain errors in training can cost dog owners years of frus-tration and sometimes can lead to an unhappy relationship with our dogs.

We all teach the basic behaviors and routines to our pups, but what happens when we go on 'auto pilot' and neglect those training classes? The response times for im-portant behaviors take longer, and in many instances our dogs do not even acknowledge us. This happens when we do not reinforce a new behavior a few times a day. Most of us will tend to go to all the puppy training classes and then presume that the training does not get forgotten. Instead, by keeping your dog's training frequent and consistent, bad habits such as jumping up on people don't occur.

Our canine companions are social animals and most en-joy jumping all over us to welcome us back home. If your dog jumps up on you, tell him to sit. This is so much more effective than punishing him. If he then makes every effort to still jump up on you, start off by greeting him from the other side of your fence or gate. Then reward him with a treat when he does sit for you. When your furry best friend does this a few times, leave the area for a few minutes and then return. This increases his level of excitement and allows for more progress in training.

Play Sit and Wait

Dogs love this game of sit and wait. When your dog greets you quietly from the gate, repeat the "sit-for-greeting " exercise from inside your gated area. Your canine companions will love practicing this and soon get the idea of what is expected of them.

This exercise needs to be practiced often over several weeks, so that the old habit of undesirable jumping up is replaced. Use a soft tone to praise and frequently reward your dog to encourage him with the desired new behavior. Never frighten him into the new behavior, but encourage him with patience and kindness.

Teach Your Dog to Go to "His Spot"

Additionally, when your guests come over to visit, teach your dog to sit on a small mat or rug. This makes it his spot where it becomes easier for him to understand what is expected of him. Why the mat? This is because the mat is a tactile object that a dog can go to and where he knows he can feel secure. Keep in mind that smaller dog breeds prefer sitting high up on chairs where they can see all the activity. Dogs are social and want to be included in all the fun!

Charlie the Pug has his own special sitting place. I jokingly refer to it as his "time-out." All I have to do is point toward the mat, and he stops what he's doing and heads on over there. Yes, sometimes he does look very much like a pouty Pug, but he does it.

Patience, time, and good training skills will usually eliminate bad behavior. To teach a pup not to jump up on young children, use a leash for correcting your pup's behavior. Then when children come to play with him and the puppy starts jumping up on them, use the "off command". This should then be followed with a small light tug on the leash. Always praise your dog when he listens and as soon as he has stopped jumping. If he starts jumping up again, repeat the process and reward for good behavior. All children must be taught not to run around dogs or encourage the pup's bad behavior. Being consistent with training is the key to success.

Destructive Chewing Types

Whoever said that dogs can do no wrong obviously never had their dogs chew up numerous pairs of shoes, or destroy favorite books. A new obsession may be your favorite Gucci loafer, or the corners of your husband's antique coffee table. Truth is though, that this can only get worse, and never improves without proper training and plenty of dog toys. To that end, be sure to train your rescue from day one. This particular bad habit can become an extremely costly one. Always remember to never get angry, no matter how much or what your dog has destroyed. A few seconds of anger can destroy all the months of bonding and trust that you both have developed together.

Puppy Chewing

Puppies chew for numerous reasons. When they are bored and need something to do, chewing occupies them. If they are teething and have sore gums, or if they have too much energy from not having enough exercise each day, chewing helps. Molding your pup's behavior by teaching him to chew on his own toys allows the problem of chewing not to become a major one. Nonetheless, there will always be a few items around the house that a puppy simply cannot resist. There are also many pups that simply have to chew and are very mouthy. Keep in mind that most behavioral problems stem from your pup being bored or feeling lonely. It is so important to spend quality time every day with your puppy, and have him around you when indoors or outdoors.

Pups are at their worst with the teething process from three to four months. Sometimes this can last for much longer. When a pup's first teeth push up through their gums at around three to four weeks, their gums hurt. Frozen ice cubes and dog lollipops from Whole Foods can bring some relief. Also freezing some carrots and Kong toys provide temporary relief during this difficult period for most puppies.

The More Destructive Chewing

Destructive chewing can be linked to diet, housebreaking, and separation anxiety. If your dog needs to go out and is unable to do so, he will become anxious and start chewing things around the house.

It took me a while to understand Max's signals. He's a Great Pyrenees, and the newest rescue. He's still very young as he's barely three years old, so he has a lot of energy. I've learned that when he starts barking and whining and doing his version of the "happy dance," it's time to go potty.

When Max's pent-up energy gets the best of him, he'll turn to a knob of furniture or anything he can mouth. This often leads to chewing. The art of distraction has become my best friend. I immediately redirect him into another activity, one that's more positive. If he continues, I pull down one of those giant dental rawhide bones to gnaw on for an hour or two. That does seem to release some of that energy, and definitely quiets him down.

Maintaining a strict schedule is key to preventing destructive chewing. Scheduling your dog's diet, when he eats, what he is eating, and how much he is eating also affects destructive chewing. Parasites, worms, and illness have also been known to cause low-grade infections that will cause your pooch to become fidgety and anxious enough to start chewing all over again. Keep in mind that when something is bothering your furry-friend, he may start chewing on something in your home. Chewing is one of the signals given by dogs.

Just like humans, dogs are prone to stress. Stress can manifest itself in a variety of ways. This is often mistaken for "bad behavior". If your rescue is exhibiting a destructive chewing behavior, the first step is always to take him to the veterinarian to ensure that there are no physical problems and that your dog is not in pain. Pain and illness can cause a dog to "act out," and behave in ways that are not like him at all. The key to getting your rescue to stop chewing is not always easy and can sometimes be frustrating. Living in the canine moment, and better understanding your new rescue enables every pet parent to understand why their furry-best friend is acting out.

Make sure that your rescue has plenty of appropriate chewable toys — Kong, Nylabone, bully stick, and even tennis balls. The Kong toy is a great substitute for a shoe and is a wonderful solution for destructive chewing. It can be easily stuffed in layers-liver paste, peanut butter and possibly cream cheese and the Kong hole can be plugged in with a healthy carrot or organic cookie. This makes for an enjoyable tasty chew toy, and will encourage your pup to gravitate towards chew toys and not your favorite books or shoes. The Kong is also super challenging and stimulating because your pup has to work to empty it of all its contents. This keeps Fido focused and out of trouble.

Frequent trips to the dog park, dog beach, and the nearby Starbucks will keep him entertained. Enroll your dog in an Agility class. There are many breed/personality-appropriate activities to indulge all dogs. Teaching your pup how to "Drop It!" when he does chew on something that he's not supposed to, and rewarding him by giving him lots of attention and a treat will reinforce positive behavior.

Introducing Your Adopted Dog to Other Dogs in the Home

Chances are that you've got other dogs living at home. I do. In this case you'll have to make some introductions. Jealousy can be avoided if you have the introductory meeting in a neutral territory, like the dog park. Let both dogs have a chance to sniff each other and play together. In time you'll be able to see if they get along. I always suggest bringing your present dog to the shelter and have someone else bring your potential rescue dog out for a walk. See if the two dogs get along or have the potential of becoming friends. This may not happen right away and you need to take this into consideration. Some dogs that have been confined for too long at a shelter have become confused and scared. This often comes out as aggression, nonetheless it normally is short-term aggression, which disappears once your dog has settled in his new home and no longer feels confused.

Be certain not to ever neglect your old dog, and always pat him first. You'll be spending a lot of time with your new dog, so bring both along for walks, or take someone with you if your new rescue is a puller, or if he reacts strangely to everything he sees.

Don't leave your dogs to their own devices until you are sure that they will get along. Dogs also team up together to get into mischief — partners in crime. In the beginning, place your new dog in his crate or in separate rooms so that you can be certain that they won't fight. Most importantly, give them plenty of playtime together to encourage bonding, so that they can become best buddies.

Introducing Your Rescue to Children at Home

As many as sixty percent of dog bite victims reported each year are children. Many of them are boys between the ages of six and nine years of age.

Dogs May Bite Children When
When they are startled by a loud noise, or being suddenly awakened;
When they feel nervous or scared;
When they get excited or are chasing after your children in a game of hide and seek;
When children press up close to hug or kiss a dog;
When children smother or hug them too tightly;
When children run around shrieking or making strange noises;
When children drag or make unusual sounds with their feet;
When dogs are in pain or are feeling sick;
When dogs have just been neutered or spayed;
When dogs have just had their vaccines;
When dogs are eating or are being fed;
When dogs are running around the dog park playing and strange children try to pat them;
When they are protecting their space, toys, blanket, pups or family;
When they have been trained to be aggressive or attack;
When kids hurt them, even unintentionally;
When there is a thunderstorm, hurricane or lightning.

Body Language of a Dog that May Bite

Most dogs will stare at you and growl. They may also hold their tails stiffly up in the air and wag it very quickly. They will show their teeth and bark, possibly but not always with their hackles up.

The term "hackles" refers to that section of hair on the dog that starts at the neck and runs down the length of the backbone all the way down the tail. The hairs stick up as a way to make the dog appear larger. You usually see it most around the shoulder and neck area. Dogs have the flight-or-fight response, and that sudden rush of adrenaline causes the hackles to rise. Often fear or aggression provoke the response. My Max raises his hackles when he sees a stray cat nearby. Charlie the Pug does it when he gets too excited during a heavy game of play with the big dogs, and he's gone a bit too far. He's a little boy compared to the large dogs but that doesn't stop him from getting into the fray. When he realizes he's taken on more than he can handle, his hackles go up. The more observant you are with your dog, the more you will understand what he is signaling, and whether that signal is a sign of fear, aggression, or a case of hyper-excitement brought on by neighborhood stray.

What to Do If You Think a Dog Is Going to Bite

Children need to stand very still and remain calm. Teach them not to scream and run. Never stare directly into his eyes and don't make any sudden moves. Then slowly back away. If a strange dog comes up to your kids and sniffs, allow him to do so. Most dogs are just curious.

If your dog is aggressive towards your children, this is a serious problem and needs to be fixed right away. Contact a dog behaviorist and your veterinarian right away. Never play rough games or tug-of-war with your dog if he is aggressive. Also keep your hands away from his head. Socialization and playing with your dog from an early age prevents aggressiveness in dogs.

Do Dogs Have Stress?

We all get nervous. So do our dogs. Your new dog may develop a few habits that can drive you crazy. This is in response to adapting to a new environment — your home. Be firm in enforcing your rules, and remember that he's not being bad. He just needs to kick a bad habit.

Some adopted dogs will venture into certain parts of your home and avoid others. Some will become boisterous and bark continuously. Educating your dog means communicating with him: helping him understand and respond to your words and actions, and you learning to respond to his signals. Dogs communicate. Take the time to become familiar with your dog and to work as a team. You'll be wonderfully surprised at how much fun you can have along the way.

Dogs of all ages must be trained. Difficult and bad habits can be hard to break. Adolescent dogs that are full of energy can have erratic tendencies. Learn how to give your dogs an outlet for their mental and physical energies. Teenage energy is best curbed with training and exercise. Older rescues do well with training, and benefit mentally from the stimulation that this provides. Training brings back your dog. Instead of having an anxious, stressed out dog, you can enjoy a calm and focused one.

Often adopted dogs find it hard to get along with other dogs in the same household. It's not unusual for them to have a few arguments to see who's top dog. Canine stress also plays into this. If you think that your adopted dog may be stressed out, and does not ever seem to relax, visit your veterinarian. Canine Prozac and other canine medications for anxiety can be prescribed and do work. Seek out a professional obedience trainer who will be able to advise on how to discourage fighting.

Furniture Climbing

Before bringing your new dog home, decide which pieces of furniture are okay for your dog to sit on. He can learn which pieces of furniture are off-limits. Some of us allow our dogs on everything and don't mind. Our furniture remains the same for years with Fido proudly claiming his favorite couch. Nonetheless, if you make a decision, stick by it, otherwise you'll confuse your dog. Use the word "Off!" and not "Down," since this will mean lie down.

Guarding Food and Toys

Keep in mind that your dog's ancestors were pack animals who had to protect their possessions from other canids in order to survive. That similar protective urge may still be in your dog. In that case you'll need to convince him that that's not necessary. He does not need to defend his toys or food.

Never taunt your dog or take things away from him in a teasing manner. Try not to take something away from him when he's busy enjoying a bone, or playing with a chew toy. Never grab something out of your dog's mouth. This would be akin to someone taking a piece of food out of our mouth while we're busy chewing. Mealtime may present a problem; so keep children and other people away from his food bowl. Place all food bowls in an area that is secluded, and that allows your dog to eat in quiet. If he loves to growl when you're nearby his dish, fill it a little at a time; stand nearby and let him eat. Wait a few seconds before filling up his bowl.

Mealtime with pups is easier. I love hand-feeding puppies so as to gain their trust and respect. Sit quietly near the food bowl and place some food in your palm. Open up your hand and feed bits. Do this throughout the puppy stage so that your puppy becomes convinced that you're not trying to steal his food. You'll never have a problem with growling or aggression during mealtimes again. You can continue doing this into adulthood. My dogs love this with homemade meals. I sometimes hand feed little bits of salmon and brown rice with broccoli, or mince, quinoa with vegetables, especially cooked for my dogs.

Nipping and Mouthing

An aggression problem with your rescue does not mean that your dog is mean or that there's a big problem. This just means that you need to work with an in-home professional trainer. Your dog needs to find out who's top dog in your home, and needs to know that he cannot use his teeth to express his anxiety or opinions. If your dog bites, you need to immediately consult with an in-home professional trainer who will be able to work with you in your home. The situation will not improve if you ignore it. Let your dog understand that you're the boss, and that no biting is allowed.

Mouthing

Mouthing is not biting. This takes place when your dog licks or lets his mouth have contact with your skin, without any intention of biting. In this case your dog would apply a soft pressure on your skin, but doesn't clamp down into your skin with his teeth. Sometimes mouthing can be a form of play. Puppies usually do this when playing with each other. Many dogs simply outgrow mouthing as they mature; yet others continue to exhibit this sometimes painful behavior throughout adulthood. This often occurs when dogs greet you at the door and are excited. It can be seen as a greeting or an invite to play.

To end mouthing, provide your dog with a chew bone or toy as soon as you return home as he starts mouthing you. If he continues mouthing, you can say "Drop!" and walk away and ignore your dog. By ignoring his behavior you're not reinforcing it, and hopefully, he will stop doing it.

Never hold your dog by the jaw and try to force it shut. This will only hurt him, and your approach should be one of gentleness in everything that you do with him. If you physically shut his mouth with your hands, you're not teaching him to inhibit himself around people, and he may continue mouthing guests and others around you for attention. Always keep an interesting selection of interactive dog toys and dog puzzles in your home to keep your furry best friend mentally stimulated at all times.

Stealing Food or Your Favorite Things

There are many dogs that love to pick up socks, shoes, and even underwear and run pell-mell around the house with it, trying to get everyone to join in on the fun and games. The solution here is simple: Let him wear his leash around the house, and when he steals something, he'll be easy to catch. Never leave a leash on an unsupervised dog.

To remove a sock or object from your dog's mouth, act fast but without scaring or hurting him: grab his snout from the top with one hand and squeeze inward on the sides (try pressing gently on his upper gums and teeth), and with the other hand reach in and extract the sock. Use the word "Give" or "Drop," then praise him when he releases his grip. If he won't unclench his jaws for even a second, try whistling close by her ear. He'll unclench his jaws for a second and you can snatch your sock away.

Teddy, HoneyBunn, Freddie, and Charlie posing.

Training Notes

Life with a Shelter Dog

So now you've adopted a shelter dog. You know that by adopting, you have to try to help him overcome any abuse or neglect that he may have endured from previous homes, or possibly from a life on the streets. You've realized that he needs training, and that it's possibly going to take longer than you thought to help him to adjust into the responsible and trained dog that you want.

There are a few common traits that often surface in adopted dogs that you'll need to keep in mind.

Submissive Dogs

This type of dog will use his body language to let the world know how deferent he is. He'll lie on his back, cower, crouch and even may have a piddle on the floor when someone pats him. The submissive dog will slink, and not prance or pound forwards, and you'll most likely see his ears pressed back against his head and of course, his tail between his legs. This type of dog has very little confidence and needs to be reassured much of the time. You'll need to let him know how wonderful he is, and to take him out as much as possible to dog parks, the beach, and on many local trips. He'll benefit from plenty of encouragement, love, and socialization. You'll need to be gentle when training him and be sure to use plenty of positive reinforcement with no physical corrections.

Many submissive shelter dogs hardly ever have eye contact. Encourage him to make eye contact: hold his head gently and speak calmly to him while looking at him. This type of dog needs to feel loved with plenty of encouragement given, and to have many play dates with other dogs. He needs to know that he can trust you and that you'll never hurt or neglect him.

Don't over cuddle or overwhelm him. It's also best to ignore certain behaviors that you don't like so as to gain his confidence. Don't reward him either for unwanted behaviors. Let him know that you are there to play and have fun, and he'll soon learn from the example you set for him. Submissive dogs do well with other dogs in the house, so encourage play. If you don't, they tend to seek out a corner and watch all the household activity from a distance.

Anxious, Worried, and Submissive Dogs

These characteristics often all tend to overlap. The anxious and worried dog is nervous about every little noise, every stranger that walks past you, and even your children. He'll look at you and then growl at his shadow in the mirror or the man wearing a hat. He hates the vacuum cleaner and becomes totally distraught when the front door slams shut.

These types of dogs need to be exposed to as many things as possible, new people and new things. If your adopted dog is a worrier, don't shelter him from the things that frighten him. Whatever you do, don't terrify him, but rather introduce him to new things and new environments every day. He should hear new noises and see things that he has never seen before.

When you introduce your adopted dog to something new at the dog park, make sure he's on a leash and does not bolt. Make each encounter fun and casual. He'll soon learn that there's nothing to be afraid of. Submission and shyness are most times not the result of abuse, but of a lack of early training and socialization with people and other dogs.

Alpha Type and Dominant Dogs

This type of dog thinks he's the leader of the pack. Dominance can be seen in small ways, from guarding his toys to grabbing the leash from you and running off. This can lead to biting other dogs or people. It's a serious problem that takes time to fix. Although dominance is common during a dog's teenage years, this tends to subside with neutering or spaying. Many shelter dogs who have grown up without training or in shelters have a hard time adapting to home life where they have to answer to someone.

By no means act aggressively towards your dog. Self-esteem and confidence are wonderful. If you are the proud parent of a dominant puppy, you can help eliminate some of these behaviors by doing a few exercises with him each day. Sit down with your puppy and pick him up. Hold him up in your arms. Next hold her close by your face, but be sure to completely support his back and body. You do this by holding him beneath his rib cage. Never hold up a dog by his shoulders. Look into your pup's eyes and coo. Talk gently to him while smiling. Your dominant pup will probably squirm trying to get out of your arms. Cradle him gently and then finally put him down. Stroke his head while with the other hand gently stroke him. This can be repeated a few times a day.

There's nothing more difficult than when going for walks when your dog keep lunging forward at people or other dogs. In this instance, let your dog know that you're the leader, and be firm about not allowing him to drag you around on walks. Your dog will improve after dog training classes.

Hyperactive and Pacing Dogs

This type of dog will make you tired. He's always running around, pacing, whining, and seems to be constantly on the go. Dogs like this need mental stimulation and plenty of exercise like agility, a game of Frisbee and long runs at the dog park. Never resort to cooping him up. This will only make matters worse. Training helps because this keeps his mind and body busy. Training classes also give him self-esteem and boost your dog's confidence. Although hyperactivity is closely related to dominance, dog training will soon teach your dog how to sit-stay and down-stay. You can use these commands when he gets too hyperactive.

Persistence, training, and patience help through these challenging times. If after training, his dominance and hyperactivity don't improve, ask yourself whether you're feeding him a properly balanced meal, or if he's eating your children's snacks. Consult your veterinarian to discuss behavioral problems that may be due to nutritional imbalances. Think about preparing homemade meals of chicken, brown rice and vegetables, or following the Raw Food Diet. Nutrition plays a large role in your dog's behavior.

Don't ever give up on Fido. Try not to think negatively. Most behavior problems can be worked through with patience and consistent training – and you may have to go through a few trainers until you find the right fit. It's the same as finding the right veterinarian or pediatrician.

Dogs are like children in that they benefit from individually tailored training packages to suit their specific needs. There is no such thing as a match that is destined to fail. You owe it to your dog to help him become a well-rounded, well-adjusted, and happy dog. Your relationship can only become stronger, but like everything good in life, you need to work at it.

Steps to a Successful Adoption

Think of adoption in this way. Can we make our dogs happy?

We know that our dogs make us incredibly happy, but before and even after we adopt, we need to ask ourselves if we're making our dogs happy by giving them a well-balanced life. Do they go to training, have appropriate veterinary care, enjoy home-cooked meals or have healthy balanced diets with plenty of raw fruits and vegetables? Do we spend enough time with them?

If your lifestyle means you will have to leave your new friend alone at home every day, make sure you choose the right breed of dog. Ask questions. Do some preliminary research on the right type of breed that can sustain long hours alone. Do whatever is necessary to make sure he doesn't get lonely or stressed from too much alone time. Yes, providing a home beats leaving him at the shelter, but you want to make sure he has the type of life he deserves.

If you find your dog is hyperactive, find out more about holistic treatments, possibly even aromatherapy massage, or the Tellington TTouch circular movement method. By incorporating Leg Circles in any dog, you're producing a pattern of movement that increases awareness. You can also do the Ear TTouches on hyper dogs to calm them down. Mouth TTouches calms and reduces stress in animals, and even reduces some emotional trauma. The TTouches deepens your connection with your dog, and helps him to trust you and relax at the same time. It's a great massage for rescues that are skittish or very stressed out.

Single Pet Parent Adoption

Adopting your new best friend will change your life. You'll make friends with other pet parents at the dog park, you'll go hiking, enjoy some great dog training classes and make many new friends.

As a single pet parent, it's best to be realistic and to consider your lifestyle. Make sure that you have plenty of free time to exercise your dog and to spend time with him. Most single-pet parents make the best canine parents. They're able to dedicate much more time to their dogs. You'll be gaining a new member to your family, and you'll be sure to never neglect your dog. As long as you're willing to make your new rescue a lifetime commitment, you'll fill that hole in your life that only a dog can fill.

If you happen to be working, you'll need a dog walker or pet sitter to walk your rescue during the day. This is definitely a better alternative than leaving your dog at home alone all day. There are also canine daycare centers that specialize in keeping your pets well exercised and happy.

The Tellington TTouch Method

Many rescues suffer from pain or memories of pain. You should always be aware that a dog in pain has the potential to snap or bite by reflex, even if he is a very docile dog. That is why when using the TTouch method you should use a muzzle. When using this method, avoid any body positions that may be threatening to your rescue. Do not lean over him or stare him directly in the eye. This method is a gentle approach to release pain and tension at the cellular level.

In 1980, when working with an Australian Sheepdog named Shawn, Linda Tellington Jones discovered that when she worked with Shawn's body, ears, and neck in order to get him to lower his head, his breathing slowed down, his stride lengthened and became more fluid. He also relaxed, and instead of barking and prancing around with his head held high, Shawn soon stopped barking. His tendency to bite was also reduced. She mentions that if you have a clear picture in your head of what you expect from your dog, dogs will "pick up" our mental pictures even when far away. The clarity of her expectations made her dogs very cooperative over the years, and made the difference between success and failure in many cases when her dogs displayed inappropriate behavior.

Today, the Tellington TTouch has developed into a popular method that is used by many trainers, dog owners, veterinarians, vet technicians, and in animal shelters all over the world. This method offers a positive, no-force approach to training, yet is much more than just a training method. It's become a way of life.

This method can help dogs who exhibit excessive barking, chewing, leash pulling, jumping up, aggressive behavior, hyperactivity, nervousness, fear-biting, timidity and shyness, resistance to grooming, fear of thunder and loud noises. This method produces permanent changes in behavior, and is great for rescues.

Follow One Golden Rule

Treat your dogs as you would like to be treated. Think positively in terms of reshaping your dog's behavior by doing so with kindness, patience, and a deep level of understanding. I like to think of it in this way. THINK LIKE A DOG. This will encourage you to have a long, healthy relationship with your furry best friend. True miracles can be accomplished when you learn how to change behaviors, including your own, in a way that positively impacts your dog's quality of life. Stay positive and kind.

My beloved Great Pyrenees Waco the Wonder Dog

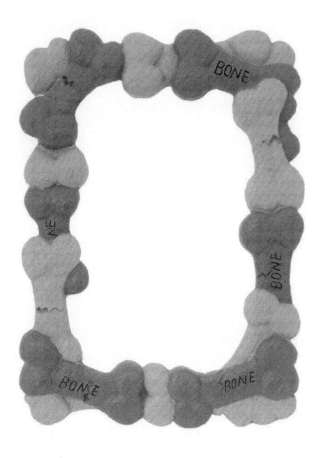

_____

_____

_____

_____

_____

_____

_____

_____

_____

_____

_____

_____

_____

_____

_____

_____

Conclusion

We are at the end of our time together. I hope that you've found this book helpful as well as inspiring and motivating. Most of all, I hope that you are ready to adopt a rescue dog.

If you have already adopted and are providing your new-found friend with his or her forever home, perhaps you will have found some encouragement and helpful information so that you and your adopted dog's bond can grow deeper.

I know the joy and happiness I've received from my adopted dogs such as Waco, the Great Pyrenees in the last photo. He's no longer with me but his presence somehow still remains and the memories stay fresh. In fact, I have now adopted Sam, who came to me by way of Waco's same foster mother.

The house is full, the joy ever-growing. May you share in the same experience when you open your home and your heart to your special rescue dog.

I also hope you'll take a look at the other books in this series: *Easy Homemade Dog Treat Recipes: Fun Homemade Dog Treats for the Busy Pet Lover* and *50 Dog Snack Recipes: Holiday Gift Ideas and Homemade Dog Treats* full of plenty of ways to show your dog your love.

Have you picked up your 27-page FREE Dog Training and Resource Guide mentioned at the front of the book? If not, please take advantage of this opportunity.

Wondering if there will be more books in this series? You bet. Visit my blog and get on my VIP list of special customers so you know in advance and grab early copies.

Thanks you,

Vikk Simmons

(*PS:* If you enjoyed this book, please leave an honest review on Amazon and on your favorite bookstore site.)

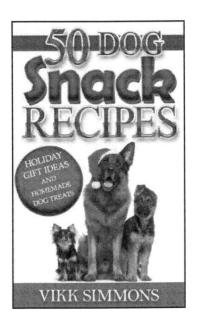

50 DOG SNACK RECIPES
Holiday Gift Ideas and Homemade Dog Treats

Book 3 in the Dog Training and Dog Care Series, *50 Dog Snack Recipes* continues the focus on those special times like holidays and special occasions where you can continue building that loving relationship with your dog through holiday gift ideas and homemade dog treat recipes. This is a great companion book to the second book in the series, *Easy Homemade Dog Treat Recipes: Fun Homemade Dog Treats for the Busy Pet Lover.*

EASY
HOMEMADE
DOG TREAT
RECIPES

WOW!
Homemade!

FUN
HOMEMADE
DOG TREATS
FOR THE
BUSY
PET LOVER

VIKK SIMMONS

EASY HOMEMADE DOG TREAT RECIPES

Book 2 in the *Dog Training and Dog Care Series*, *Easy Homemade Dog Treat Recipes - Fun, Homemade Dog Treats for the Busy Pet Lover*, focuses on building that loving relationship with your dog through cooking and having fun, while sharing pet-safe, treats for love and for training with your beloved dog. Great companion book to *50 Dog Treat Snacks*.

No Oven! No Problem! No Cook Dog Treats
Canine Cookies
Doggie Biscuits
Pupcakes
Easy directions
Special Treats for Senior Dogs
Dehydrated Dog Treats
Training Treats
Doggie Biscuits
Special Treats for Hypoallergenic Dogs
Special Treats for Wheat Intolerant Dogs
Special Treats for Problems (fleas, bad breath, etc.)

About the Author

The author and her granddaughter meeting Waco the Wonder Dog for the first time and ready to take him home

As I mentioned early on, I have a passion for dogs, all dogs, but rescue dogs hold a special place in my heart.

Dogs can become wonderful companions. All you have to do is open your heart and let them in. With love, time, attention, and training, the relationship will grow, and the bond will be affirmed many times over.

Having lived a dog-filled life from the day I was born, I can testify to the enormous gift each and every dog has brought into my life.

Over the years I've spent my share of time training the dogs that have come into my care. I've studied with a dog trainer, taken lessons, and reached out to those with way more knowledge than I will ever have. I've read the books and articles and watched the videos. Most of all, I've lived with dogs, filled my day with dogs, and watched the dogs.

Being observant provides a wealth of insight about dogs and their individual habits and needs. In addition, I've lived with a wide range of breeds from the wonderful no-pedigree mutts to the specific breeds from German Shepherds, Great Pyrenees, American Cocker Spaniels, Pugs, Maltese, Beagles, to the newer, developing Mi-Kis.

Rescues come in all stripes. Join us in a pack-filled life.

Vikk Simmons

Let's Connect!

Like most authors, I'm delighted to hear from my readers. You can find me online through a variety of ways:

Visit my blog A Life with Dogs
www.ALifeWithDogs.com.

Follow my Amazon Author Page
amazon.com/author/vikksimmons

Like and join my A Life with Dogs Facebook Page.
https://www.facebook.com/A Life with Dogs

Follow me on Twitter @PackLeader_Vikk

Excerpt Introduction

Making your own homemade dog treats for your furry companion is a wonderful way for you and your family to bond with your dog. It's also a good way of making sure you know exactly what goes into your dog's diet – no nasty additives, or crazy amounts of sugars that will have Rover bouncing off the walls for hours on end, or even ultimately harm your pet over time.

There are so many different types of dog treats that you can make yourself that are nutritious and delicious and make for wonderful training bribes.

Making homemade dog treats is a safe way of treating dogs with special dietary requirements, whether they are a new puppy, athletic, diabetic, overweight, and wheat-intolerant or a senior with specific needs. You'll never realize how much better your dog treats are for your pet until you make them. Once you've whipped up a batch of treats yourself, do compare the ingredients to the shop-bought treats. You won't want to go back.

Why is a homemade treat that much better for your dog? Have you ever read through all the ingredients in store bought treats? Do you even have the slightest idea what you're feeding your family pet? You won't have to worry once you use the dog treat recipes that follow. You know every ingredient that goes into your dog's belly.

You might be surprised to learn that homemade dog treats are much cheaper than the overpriced store-bought stuff. Go ahead. Try the recipes. You'll be delighted at how much money you can save – while still spoiling your best buddy.

The do-it-yourself process of making dog treats is pretty simple. Create a list of the ingredients you're going to need and pick them up next time you're at the grocery store. I like to have the pantry stocked so I can bake a batch of biscuits any time one of the dogs gives me that *look*. (You know the one, the pouty hang-dog look.) A well-stocked pantry allows me the freedom to try the recipes whenever I want. In chapter 4, I've included a handy list of ingredients to add to your shopping list.

Many recipes in this collection are quick and easy, while others need a half hour or so to bake. Need something super easy? Check out the no-oven, no-cook recipe section. Be sure you review all the preparation and storage tips. They will help you save time and ensure that you keep enough tasty tidbits on hand for several weeks at a time.

Is your dog gluten or wheat intolerant? Does your dog have allergies? What about obesity? Our dogs are as prone to this disease as we are. All of this is covered in the additional healthy treat ideas and the allergies and special dietary needs section. You'll find a quick list of wheat flour substitutes as well as the standard substitutions and a basic hypoallergenic dog treat recipe.

What's my favorite part of this entire homemade dog treat thing? My dogs. I love to see those eager, loving faces, and drooling mouths that greet me at treat time. Once you start making your own homemade dog treats, you may never buy store-bought treats again. Let's face it: Not only are homemade treats delicious and nutritious; they are full of love.

Buy EASY HOMEMADE DOG TREAT RECIPES today.

www.amazon.com/dp/B00QDAQ4G0

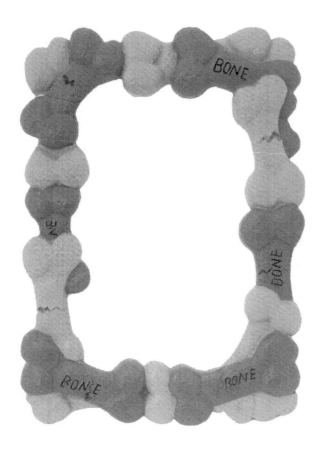

_____

_____

_____

_____

_____

_____

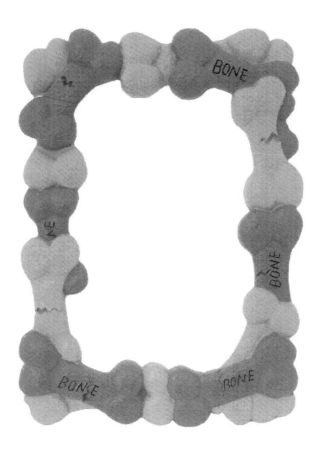

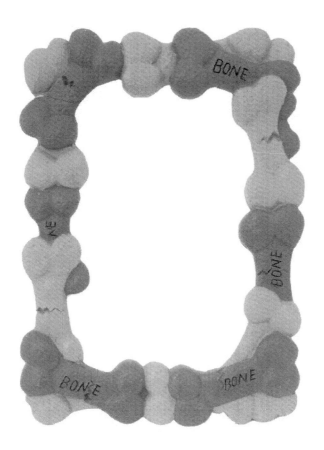

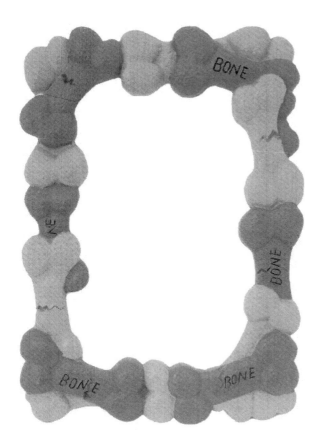

Index

Made in the USA
Monee, IL
01 November 2019